Blessed

A Journey of Miracles in Africa

By

Jean-Luc Lézeau

All rights reserved. No part of this book may be reproduced or transmitted in any form or by any means without written permission from the author.

Copyright ©2023 by Jean-Luc Lézeau

From the same author:

« **Strategic Church Finances: A Biblical Approach**" by Jean-Luc Lézeau and Benjamin C Maxson. Stewardship Department of the General Conference of SDA.2008

« **The Abundant life** » Serie of 50 of 30mn program. Stewardship Department of the General Conference of SDA.2009
https://www.youtube.com/@gestionchretiennedelaviepa6246

« **The Abundant Life** » 2012. JLL Publishing.

Contents

Prologue	1
Good Start?	7
Lukanga	23
Ad Interim	27
Going to Market	33
Meanwhile	39
School rebellion	43
New Year in Korora	51
A Switchover	57
Songa	59
Head Wound	63
Extra Vacation in Lusaka	69
Visit in the Middle of the Bush	75
Yearend Grades	77
See you next time or adios?	81
Cameroon	87
Douala	91
Moving	111
Back to France	119
Beating the Inflation	129

Language Courses 131
Angola and Mozambique 139
Epilogue 147
Acknowledgment 153

Prologue

I never knew my father. I was born three months after he was killed in the famous battle of Monte Cassino near Rome during World War II. My father was a medic in the Army. He did not really have a choice: the status of conscientious objector was unknown at the time, and enlistment was required for everyone, pastor or not, as was his case.[1] Not wanting to bear arms, he opted for the best way to help his fellow men: to be a medic. After saving several of his fellow soldiers, he was wounded and died on the battlefield.

That idealistic picture of a father who

---

[1] Antoine Paul Lézeau was a pastor in Algeria at the time.

worked in a foreign land and gave his life to save others was what motivated me to become a missionary.

A rendering of a Medic on a battlefield. Desmond Ford Memorial. Collegedale, Tennessee.

Years later, my wife Eileen and I received our first call: to teach in our secondary school in Lukanga, Zaire.[2] We were eager to discover where that was. At

---

[2] Now the Democratic Republic of Congo.

the time Google Earth did not exist, and we had to look at an Atlas to find where Lukanga was. In fact, it was so small that we could not find it on the map (to this day it does not show up on Google Earth). We were told that the nearest town was Butembo, which was not on the map either.[3] Goma was the only town large enough to be mentioned, but that was 300 km (185 miles) away! Welcome to nowhere! The second discovery we made was that there are a surprising number of schools, hospitals, and mission stations around the world that are located in places that are almost impossible to reach.

I also soon discovered that serving as

---

[3] It is only recently that Butembo shows up on Google Maps.

missionary was like enlisting into the French army. After basic training, the Sergeant asks each recruit: "What trade have you trained for?" If the answer was mechanic, he was assigned to work in the kitchen. If the answer was baker, he ended up as a truck driver, and so on. Similarly, I was asked to teach all kinds of subjects except the one I was qualified to teach. I soon learned that a professor had to be two lessons ahead of his students.

To be somewhat prepared for the cultural shock, we attended the first Mission Institute held outside the United States by Drs: Gottfried Oosterwal and Russell Staples. It was a month-long seminar which took place at Newbold College in Binfield, England.

Dr. Oosterwal on the far-left and Dr Staples on the far-right.

Good Start?[4]

Our journey to Africa started on Thursday, September 4, 1975, at 6:40 a.m. at the railway station in Thonon les Bains, France, where we lived. We arrived at the station in Paris Gare de l'Est at 1:30 p.m. and took a taxi to Roissy airport to fly to Brussels, from where we would then fly to Kinshasa, the capital of Zaire. We could have flown out from Geneva, Switzerland, which is only 40 km from Thonon, but apparently somebody had decided that it would be too easy for a family with two small

---

[4] The first two chapters of this book were published on May 24, 2012 in Adventist Review©

children to start their missionary service that way.

Our baggage allowance enabled us to carry essential items we would need to live on for the next 3 months while waiting for our crate. Eileen and I, with our two children aged 3 and 4, checked our three metal trunks and our two suitcases prior to boarding our aircraft. We arrived in Brussels on time and queued up to board our connecting Sabena flight. To our surprise, we were told that our missionary tickets would not allow us to take that airline! Pleading that all our luggage were checked to Kinshasa, that we had nothing with us, and that we had two small children with us was…of no avail. The agent told us that the only solution was to put our names on the waiting list for the next Air Zaire flights, which were full. Our journey to nowhere started well and our resolve to serve in the mission field faltered in our hearts. Was it really God's plan for us to go to Africa? What were we supposed to do? I had just graduated from university, had not received my first paycheck, and in fact, I had no idea at all how much I would get paid. It was not the type of question to ask when leaving as a missionary, and now I was supposed to find a hotel in one of the most expensive towns in Europe! We took the train downtown to the local Conference office and explained our situation to the treasurer. He called the Division and quickly changed our tickets and found a hotel for us. The next day, we took off in good spirits to continue our trip and discover where Lukanga was. Our enthusiasm soon cooled off when, after waiting most of the day—no time to shop for some essentials in town—we were told that the first flight was full, as well as the second and the third one! The procedure had to be repeated the following day! By that time, I had phoned the treasurer to make sure our room was still available in the hotel, and we spent our second night in Brussels. The following day, a Friday, we were told that at long last an aircraft with four seats was available and leaving that night.

When talking about our predicaments to passengers on the flight and learning that our trunks and suitcases had been flown to Kinshasa three days before, they all told us not to bother to check on them at the airport…they would all be gone. Needless to say, hearing this did not lift our spirits very much. Here we were with two small children, wearing the same clothes for the third consecutive day; we had not yet started our ministry, and we had already lost everything we owned and were still wondering where Lukanga was!

After a 12-hour flight, we landed at N'jili airport in Kinshasa la belle (the beautiful), capital city of Zaire on the west coast of the continent. The first impression you get when the plane door opens is the smell and the heat wave that hit you right in the face as you climb down the stairs. The temperature was about 40° C. Despite the warnings that we received on the plane, we went and presented our luggage stubs to a Sabena ground crew who directed us to another building since they had supposedly arrived three days earlier. To our perfect surprise and delight, our three trunks were still there, apparently untouched! We were so thankful for God's care. In a country where stealing and corruption are a way of life, it was a real miracle that our luggage was there waiting for us.

As the Belgian Conference Treasurer knew that we were leaving the night before, we expected him to have sent a message for someone from the mission to be waiting for us. But nobody was there. True, it was Sabbath, but being first-time missionaries with two children…we still expected a welcome party. The trouble was that I knew that Goma was just across the country, only two thousand kilometers away, but we only had a flight ticket to Kinshasa. How were we supposed to fly to Goma?

We found a taxi, loaded our trunks and suitcases, and asked the taxi driver to drive us to the Adventist Mission. He gave no indication that he hadn't heard of our church before and had no idea where it was situated in a city which had more than one million inhabitants at the time. By that time, we were all so thirsty and our children were crying for a drink. Meanwhile the taxi driver drove us into town and stopped from place to place to ask if anybody knew where the Adventist church was! We even went to the French

Embassy to enquire about our church. They sent us to the nearest Church of Christ!

Our trip lasted three hours and when someone was finally able to give us directions, we found the one and only small Adventist church in the whole town. It was the end of the service. Thank God, Pastor Célicourt from Haiti took control of the situation from then on. He asked a Zairian brother to negotiate the taxi fare knowing full well that we would be ripped off if I, the *musungu* (white man), had asked the price. We soon learned that nobody had heard anything about our arrival and that the local mission had neither a hotel reservation nor a flight ticket for us. What a nice, planned trip to nowhere!

The next step was to find a place to stay until our brethren could secure airline tickets for us. In a capital city where hotels are numerous but expensive, missionaries usually use guest rooms in Protestant facilities. Unfortunately, they were full for that night, but we did make a reservation for the following nights. The only solution left for us was to find a regular hotel for one night. After visiting several with no vacancies, the only solution opened to us was to "negotiate" a room. This is the third discovery we made in Africa: you can "negotiate" almost anything… especially a red light!

At the next hotel we went to all the rooms were booked, but if we paid a little extra, one could be made available! We had been travelling for more than 28 hours, we were worn out, sweating from all our pores, and I will not describe our children. We settled on the amount and went upstairs, thankfully, to our air-conditioned room. What came out of the shower, however, was just a trickle of brownish-colored water that we had to make do with before collapsing on our beds, completely exhausted. It was only the next day that we realized that the sheets we had slept in had not been changed before our arrival.

The next morning our good Haitian friend came to fetch us and give us a lift to the Protestant mission. We would stay in that guest house for a week waiting for our ticket to Goma to be "negotiated" by the local mission. However, in our haste to leave that expensive, not so clean hotel, Eileen forgot her brand-new raincoat in the hotel room. It was already late afternoon by the time she realized it. We explained the situation to the man in charge of the guest house and asked him to call a taxi for us. With a sad smile on his face, he told us that it was probably a waste of time and money to go to the hotel because, for sure, the raincoat would not be found. After the ordeal we had been through during the week, it was the last straw for Eileen. She prayed in her heart: "Lord if you really want me to stay in this country and serve you, please let me find my raincoat."

We went to the hotel and despite the fact that the room had been "cleaned," lo and behold, her raincoat was still hanging behind the door waiting for her! Miracle. Did you say miracle? God used that raincoat to tell us that He really wanted us to be there. It was our first day in the mission field out of the eleven years we were to spend in Africa.

We did arrive in Lukanga. It took a week of "negotiating" with the travel agent to find four seats for Goma and another round of "negotiating" at the airport, because having a ticket didn't give you the right to board the plane on Air Zaire (most often called "Air Maybe"

["Air Peut-être"] because nobody knew for sure when the flight would be leaving, if there was a pilot who happened to be there, or if the jet had a full tank when it took off. We did finally arrive in Goma…but we were missing a suitcase.

Claude Sabot, an old schoolmate from Collonges, was waiting for us at the airport. He was the principal of Lukanga Secondary School, which had a burgeoning seminary under the direction of Dr. Elton Wallace.

We spent the weekend at the mission waiting until Wednesday for our trunks to arrive. But one suitcase was missing![5]

---

[5] It was on December 18th during Eileen's birthday party that Claude offered her a present: the suitcase that he had brought back from Goma the day before! It took 66 days to recover a suitcase…and you say that French

Claude had already spent many years in Algeria, Madagascar, and Zaire, so we felt we were in good hands. That did not prevent him from driving his car into a ditch on the way to Lukanga.

It was true that it was the rainy season, and the dirt road was slippery. The road went through Rwankeri game reserve, and while waiting on the road for another car to stop and help us pull our vehicle

---

administration is terribly slow?

back on the road, we had the chance to see a couple of Okapi that were grazing nearby. They are exceedingly rare, and it was the only time that we saw these animals in our eleven years in Africa! Maybe God used them to give us a wink by saying: "You see, in the middle of all your woes, you are privileged to see a rare species of my creation. I have asked them to be right there just for you."

We arrived at Lukanga, the mystical mission station on September 16—12 days after our departure from Thonon.

Lukanga

Arriving on campus, we were met by half a dozen missionaries from Canada, the United States, and Belgium.

The senior of us all was Elton Wallace who had been a missionary in Viet-Nam and South Africa. He was starting a theology department which is still, to my knowledge, the only one in the Democratic Republic of Congo today. Later on, he went to Ruhengeri, Rwanda, to do the same, thanks to his abilities to raise funds in the U.S.

There was no electricity. A thunderstorm had struck the generator the previous night, as if to celebrate our arrival.

The next day, we went to the nearest

town, Butembo, to purchase the few supplies we could find. On the way back, we got stuck in the mud five times. Tim Korson, Elton Wallace, and I were the slaves who had to push the car out of the mud while Claude gave us directions! It is true that it was his car, he was the principal and was becoming an expert at getting his car out of the mud, do you see a problem?

We had to wait 9 days for the generator to be fixed and enjoy 2 hours of electricity per night.

As far as our belongings were concerned, at a time when containers did not yet exist, we were told to pack all of our belongings into one big crate to prevent theft since it had to be shipped through Mombasa (Kenya) before going by train to the Zairian border by way of Uganda. That is only half of the African continent, folks! Our goods followed the indicated route but arrived 8 months later! If unloading such a crate from the boat to a rail car was not a problem in Mombasa, we got lucky at the end of the rail track that somebody had the idea to slide the crate onto a waiting truck bed. But what our brethren at the Division did not know was that at the end of the journey, in Beni, there was no crane big enough to lift a crate of such a size. So, they pushed it down from the back of the truck—and it opened like an egg! When we discovered our belongings, they were piled up like in a pyramid in the corner of a shed. Nothing was missing, and only one glass was broken.

Do you still not believe in miracles?

The Lukanga missionary families in 1975. From left back to front: Tim Korson, Claude Sabot, Jean-Luc and Eileen Lézeau, Pr. Célicourt, Averil and Laren Kurtz, Evelyn and Elton Wallace, Diane Korson, Jean-Philippe Lézeau, Philippe and Farida Sabot, in front of Farida: Eric and Luc Sabot, Fred and Kathy Christiansen. In front: Sandrine Lézeau.

Ad Interim

I had just finished teaching a full year of subjects foreign to me, when Claude Sabot announced that he was leaving for Canada to pastor a local church, so I was asked to step in as ad interim principal, "préfet" in the local terminology. Some would consider it a promotion, but frankly, when I was asked if I would be willing to fill the position, I was not at all comfortable with it. I had never worked behind a desk before. I was a manual guy: I liked to work with my hands. When the Adventist Volunteer Service was first started in the summer of 1969 in the Euro - Africa Division, I was the first volunteer to go to Africa to build churches and missionary housing. The work of administration was as foreign to me as what was happening on the moon. That is what I replied to the brethren. The Union President insisted on two arguments: 1. I was the only French person who knew the Belgian educational system well enough to be able to talk to the local educational authorities in fluent French, and 2. I was not to worry since it was only temporary. The Union had called a Zairian, Brother Ntaganda, who was finishing his masters at Andrews to the position, and he was supposed to arrive before the new school year started. In other words, do not think that the promotion that you are going to have is based on your own merit! The color of your passport may have something to do with that![6]

On these premises, I accepted the responsibility. Little did I know that I had started on a new adventure in a world unknown to me: school and church finances, which were going to be part of my ministry for the next 25 years! It was a few months later that I met Dick Roos who was going to open my eyes to the unique ways that God provides us with opportunities to discover and develop gifts that He has given us...if we are humble enough to be a tool in His hands. I am a living example of that. But that does not mean that the road is going to be easy!

---

[6] At the time, the French was light blue, compared to the American one which is deep blue.

As soon as I accepted the position, the Union called Br. Kalume, the only accountant on campus, to go to Songa, a mission hospital in the South. Suddenly not only was I the interim "préfet," but I was also the accountant and treasurer of the institution. All for the same salary, of course! This is a joke, folks. I never expected a bonus of any kind, since those working for the church know that your salary is never affected by the many hats that you have to carry—later I would have five different ones. In fact, I was never told in advance what my salary would be before leaving for Zaire. It was not the kind of question that new missionaries would ask at the time. Eileen and I would soon discover that the first salary that we received would barely pay for the bag of wheat that we could get in Butembo, the nearby town. Your choice was to purchase it when it was available or wait for the next shipment—that might never come.

Going back to my story, the Union auditor had to come to the school and give me a crash course on accounting. It was Bob Lemon, future treasurer of the General Conference. It was Bob who taught me the difference between a debit and a credit. First the color of the voucher, red and yellow, then the difference, or rather the balance, that should always exist in the accounting system between the left and the right columns of the ledger. And if the two did not match it meant that I made a mistake somewhere. Another lesson that Bob taught me was that I could manipulate the numbers according to certain rules to make sure that they would balance—but this is not something that can be done with people. At the time, I think I heard a kind of regret in his voice.

Since then, I can vouch for the fact that what he said was the truth.

Going to Market

In the meantime, I had to prepare for the next school year. North Kivu, where Lukanga school is located, is a very fertile region at 4,500 ft (1.300 m) of altitude and situated on the Equator. You need only to drop a seed and a bush will grow without you doing anything else. That is why it is almost impossible to understand why we could not find local staples for the boarding students. No need to say that for foreigners, it was even more difficult.

Do not try to find your favorite brand of ingredients in Butembo…sometimes the only choice of food on the shelves was baked beans…or more baked beans!

Nothing else. The shopping experiences of our missionary sisters were quite short-lived. However, I was told that even Goma, the largest town in the East of Zaire where we landed, was not big enough to find sufficient drums of palm oil, beans, and other local staples; the nearest large market was Kisangani. It was 720 km (450 miles) away on a dirt road! When we arrived in Zaire in 1975, we were told that the paved roads were around 120 km (75 miles) long, in a country three times the size of France or Alaska. After having visited the country quite a bit I can assure you that nobody knows where these paved roads were. It is only after visiting the largest towns: Kinshasa, Lubumbashi, Kisangani, and Bukavu—that I realized that they must have counted the paved roads inside these cities twice—once going, the other coming back—in order to arrive at that figure!

In fact, if I had consulted the local tourist guide that I bought upon arrival, I would not have had to wonder. It was plainly marked in red: the only paved road in Zaire!

The paved roads are in red! You just have to make the difference between red and orange. Easy enough, no?

And as far as I know, this is probably true of all former French-speaking colonies. If road systems were built, very few were paved.

We must remember that the Belgian Congo was the private property of the King of Belgium, although Rwanda, on the other hand, was a Belgian colony. (In 1960, when the Belgian Congo became independent, there was only one Congolese graduate student in the whole country.) That did not change the fact that they were colonized the same way—with very poor infrastructure. That is also true for all former French colonies.

However, as soon as you cross the border into an English-speaking country, you have a paved road that welcomes you through the whole country.

I left with Paul, the English-speaking truck driver, as he was originally from Uganda, and a motor boy.[7] We took the school truck to Kisangani. It took us two days and one night. I drove part of the way to relieve Paul who was first genuinely concerned about my abilities to drive the truck, but after a couple of hours, he relaxed and could take a rest until his next shift. We left Kisangani with a truckload full of goodies just to find out, hours after we left, that a drum of oil was leaking we had already lost half of it along the way! And the motor boy had never seen a thing!

---

[7] A motor boy does everything that is below the status of a truck driver. Loads the truck, digs it out of the mud, and he is allowed to sit on top of the goods piled up on the back of the truck.

Meanwhile

It became clear that the famous Brother Ntaganda whom everybody was waiting for was not going to come.

The next experience we lived had nothing to do with food. I wish it had been. The school year had started with the Wallaces, Korsons, Kurtzs, the newlywed Christiansen, Robert Dick, and a few new additions to our missionary family: Eddy Johnson and his family, Pastor Celicourt, and the Ahlers.

The Ahlers had been told by the General Conference that a brand-new mission house would be waiting for them when they arrived. Unfortunately, it was they who had to wait for a couple of months since their house foundation had just been started!

To start the school year, the General Conference sent us Dr. Daniel Walther, a Swiss professor retired from the Theological Seminary at Andrews University, who had been the director at Collonges when my father was a theology student. It was an odd choice since he had never in his life worked abroad, only in Europe and in the U.S.

The day he arrived he asked if he could call his wife. It was a bit awkward to tell him that phones did not exist in that part of the world. Our only connection to the outside world was via short-wave radio with the Union every morning at 6:00 am.

Later on in the afternoon, we showed him the campus and had a meeting in the school to talk about the beginning of the school year. As the meeting dragged on and it was past 5:00 p.m., he stood up to switch the lights on…only to discover that he had to wait until 7:00 p.m. for the generator to be turned on—and then for only 2 hours!!!

A few days later he borrowed the school Toyota Landcruiser because he needed to get out a bit. His outing lasted only one hour as he realized that there was nowhere to go except to ride along the dirt road, which was full of potholes. He left a few days later, as the conditions we were living in were not to his liking at all.

School rebellion

Bro. Ntaganda was a Tutsi, and that distinction did not make any difference to me at the time. But I was soon to learn what tribalism means in Africa. If you have not heard of it before, let me introduce it to you. An African's first allegiance is to his family, then to his tribe, then to his country.

This was sadly shown in the 1994 Rwanda genocide where thousands of Tutsis were killed—sometimes with the help of some "God-fearing Christians." Tutsis were a minority (14%) in Rwanda, but have been the ruling tribe for decades, thanks to Belgian colonialism. They were entitled to education and government positions to enforce Belgian rules over the Hutus who were left behind. In 1959, for the first time, the Hutus rebelled against both the colonial power and the Tutsis who were trying to maintain their power. A horrific genocide happened, and over 200,000 Tutsis migrated to the nearby Belgian Congo. Since then, almost every decade has seen armed rebellions taking place in this country, each time with Tutsis taking refuge in nearby countries. In the meantime, the Belgian Congo had become Zaire.

It is in this context that we lived in 1976. The majority of our students were Tutsis—and they were all expecting Ntaganda to "liberate them" from the colonialists' missionaries.

Although the school year started as it

should, Dr. Walther's episode gave the Tutsi students the feeling that their brother from Andrews was not coming back. That was a blow for them.

The excuse for the delay was that he was finishing his master's degree. However, a few months after the school finished, we received words that he had decided to stay in the U.S. Ntaganda was the first sponsored Zairian student that the Trans-Africa Division sent to Andrews for further studies. And unfortunately, he would start a long list of sponsored students who would not go back to their country to serve the church that had helped them. That would explain later the creation of Church universities on various continents. Trying to uproot someone "only for a few years" for further education in the hope that he will come back to his country to help his brother…does not work.

To show their discontent the students formed a rebellion against the missionaries. It started in the evening when they came from their dormitories armed with big sticks and machetes, surrounded the missionaries' houses, and started pelting our house with stones. One went through our children's bedroom window as they were lying in their beds. To protect them, we had to bring Jean-Philippe and Sandrine into the corridor as far away as possible from the windows to be protected on both sides by the walls. Jean-Philippe and Sandrine, although just children, got down on their knees and prayed that God would protect all the missionaries. Such childlike faith was beautiful to see.

Unfortunately, it was a situation we would have to go through again, but under other circumstances.

The students broke into the Kurtz' house armed with machetes and were running after them. Fortunately, the couple who had just had their first baby managed to lock themselves in the bathroom for protection.

Instead of hiding, I went out and joined Elton Wallace who was trying to calm and reason with the students. But after a few stones were thrown at us, I grabbed a big stick from our wood pile and started going after them and hitting the few who were not quick enough to run away. I am sure that they were surprised by my reaction and that a good Christian would retaliate against them and even use a weapon against them. Even Elton was shouting at me to calm down.

By that time, the nearby villagers had come and stayed the rest of the night on campus with lighted torches to protect us. That is how we got acquainted with the Nandi people, who are the local natives, and did not appreciate the Tutsi interference in local affairs. The Nandis stayed the rest of the night, and we did not see Tutsis anymore that night.

The next day, when the local authorities came to assess the situation, Elton insisted that I show my back, which was marked by a blow I received during our fight, to show that we were not only talking about an exchange of words during our battle. It was a small "consolation" to me when I noticed the next day that a student had a bandage around his head. Nobody asked him, but it would have been hard for him to say that he did not have anything to do with what happened the previous night. Doesn't the Old Testament talk about an "eye for an eye"? In that case, it was a back for a head. I am still wondering if the student with the bandage learned something from this experience.

New Year in Korora

To break the monotony of student rebellion, searching for food, learning how to differentiate between pink (credit) and yellow (debit) vouchers, etc., we accepted the invitation to go on a trip with the Kurtzes for the New Year. At the time they were the only missionaries who had a private car, a 4L (R4) Renault. They took us to Korora in Rwanda which was a church camping area on the shore of Lake Kivu.

Two things happened that made our trip memorable. As our holiday was to last only 2 or 3 days, we had taken the minimum of clothes with us: we were 4 adults in the car plus two children and a baby! If you are not versed in French cars, I can tell you that the trunk of a 4L(R4)[8] Renault is quite small, and not meant for 6 people at all!

It was my first experience of an African-like trip when it is not unusual to be squeezed between a big mama and some other travelers' goats or chickens next to you on the train—or even in an airplane.

Korora was a nice property with several bungalows. We met with other missionaries working in Rwanda, especially in their school in Gitwe. The bungalows had the bare minimum and were quite small, we left our shoes outside not to mess up the small place.

The next day after our arrival, as I got

---

[8] 4L(R4) does not mean 4 people on the left and 4 people on the right!

up after a little siesta to recuperate from our various adventures, I searched for my shoes…and I am still looking for them! They were gone. I had to borrow a pair of spare sandals Laren Kurtz gave me for the rest of the trip.

Almost the same thing happened to Elton Wallace. One day he was looking for a pair of shoes in his home on the Lukanga campus but could not find them. After a while he asked the student help he had in his home if he took them, his answer was straightforward: "Yes, Sir." "Why did you take them?" "Because I need them, Pastor. You do not, you have twelve pairs and I have none. You keep preaching about God's love and how we should love one another, so I thought that you would not mind." Elton had to go in his closet to check it out, but it was true that he had 12 pairs of shoes, then 11, and had never realized it before. What could he say? On top of that, he was the head of the Bible school which he had just started! In fact, we discovered that nothing is really stolen in Africa, it is just "displaced." The student had just displaced the shoes from Elton's closet to his. Was that a big deal?

The second memorable event that happened was on the second night as we were relaxing by the lake. The sky was illuminated by the Nyiaragongo volcano, which had just erupted across the lake. We learned later that it was one of the most dangerous active volcanoes on earth and that the lava can descend into the valley at a speed of 100 km/h. As the volcano is situated only 20 km on the west side of Goma, the main question for us was whether the lava covered the road we had to take to drive back to Lukanga. As you know by now, the number of roads available for use in that part of the world was extremely limited. The only way to find out was to leave early the next morning and see for ourselves. Fortunately, the road was still open, and we reached Lukanga safely. That did not last too long because a few days later, it was impossible to send a truck to Goma. The road had disappeared under the lava, which made our following experience even more interesting.

A Switchover

I do not know if it was the student rebellion or my struggle with accounting that triggered the Union to initiate a switch in leadership. However, early one morning in January, the Union decided to call Dick Roos, who was principal at Songa secondary school, to come over to Lukanga and ask me, after asking Laren Kurtz who turned it down, to go down to Songa to be manager-director of the whole mission station—a switch over.

Since the Nyiragongo volcano had cut the road, we were left with the mission planes to move our families between these two mission stations, which were 1,100 km apart. That may be relatively easy for a couple, but with two children, we had a little more stuff to move. Remember when we received our crate? Just over 6 months before, after waiting 8 months for it to get there!

At the time there were three missionary planes and we were assured that part of our goods would be loaded on each flight going South until everything would be moved. To cut the story short, 18 months later we were still waiting for some of our goods to be shipped, and we never saw some things, including a rug carpet that we had purchased from a departing missionary!

Songa

Songa is one of those mission stations lost in the middle of nowhere. On an old map which was pinned on the school wall, Songa was mentioned as well as the surrounding villages. It must be said that it was the only hospital with over one hundred beds in this Southern part of the country. And at the time the villages were populated enough to be mentioned on the map. The nearest town Kamina was 80 km (50 miles) away. But since then, the Zairians, like most village people everywhere in the world, had moved to the nearest town to look for jobs and a better way of life. Only old people were left in the villages. If the need for a hospital made sense at the beginning of the century, now we had to get the patients from the nearest train station 15 km (9 miles) away or even to Kamina. This goes well when you have the vehicles and the gas to do so, but at one time, we only had the school tractor that was running. For a while it was the local taxi! Then we had problems with the generator, as well, and we went several weeks without electricity. The doctors in the hospital could do surgery only when the sun was shining, and we had to use our wood stove to sterilize their equipment.

Need a ride to the train station?

Locally approved sterilization equipment

A little friend, sort of, waiting for us on our porch.

Part of the missionary family at Songa. Sr. Evert, Eileen with our two kids, Dr. Suzelle Vieilledent, a volunteer nurse from the state, Monica a nurse from Barbados, and Sr. and Dr. Rohee.

Head Wound

In Songa we only had two forms of entertainment: the small river down the road from the mission and volleyball.

The river was our first choice on Sunday when all missionaries walked down with their children to spend the day in the shade near the river.

At the river there were three things that we could do. The first one was the picnic and that was the affair of the sisters. However, what attracted mainly men and their sons was to walk a good distance up the river and then float down on an innertube. It was quite enjoyable. You had to be careful to stay in the middle of the stream in order not to be caught by the tree branches which were on both sides of the sinuous river. I did enjoy it until one day, as I was floating down, I noticed a 6-foot-long water snake that was sliding down a tree trunk into the river. Apparently, it was an inoffensive one, but I chose not to mention it to the women in order to avoid a general panic.

The courageous ones, however, would climb a tree on the side of the river and jump in the pool at the foot of the waterfall. Dr. Olavi Rouhe, a retired American surgeon of Finnish origin, who was over 70 years old, was daring enough to do it. All the parents had a hard time telling their boys that it was not a good idea without offending the dear doctor!

The second was a game of volleyball that was played almost every day before sunset with some teachers, nurses, and missionaries. As it was the only entertainment of the day, (remember no TV or iPhones over there at the time), while some played the rest were watching and cheering the players. Our son Jean-Philippe was sitting under a mango tree to watch the game. Unfortunately, it was the bad season of the year to sit there: the mangos were ripe and were tempting to some of the children. As they were too small to climb the tree, they were throwing stones or, in that case, broken bricks to make the mangos fall. I do not recall if they got a lot of mangos. What I remember is that Jean-Philippe was at the receiving end of one of the bricks!

It was a wound that was big enough that it needed to be stitched up. However, as it was a period where we did not have electricity and it was already too dark, we had to wait until the following day for the doctor to look at him. We managed to stop the bleeding with a big bandage around Jean-Philippe's head and the next morning Dr. Rouhe was waiting for him in the theater. As I said before, he was in his seventies, but what I did not say is that he had the beginnings of Parkinson's disease. Jean-Philippe was ready to go ahead without local anesthesia, which the hospital did not have at the time. However, when Eileen saw the needle in the trembling hands of Dr. Rouhe approaching Jean-Philippe's head, she fainted. Instead of one patient, the hospital treated two that morning!

One memorable moment was when a patient who had a back injury was transported on a bicycle from Kisangani. I don't know how his helpers managed to make an 1850 km (1,145 miles) journey with him. It took them weeks, only to be told that there was nothing that the surgeon could do to help him. The hospital was not equipped for orthopedic procedures. Doctors could only relieve his pain and were not optimistic at all as his situation worsened. Thanks to the caring doctors and nurses who were praying daily for him, however, he gave his heart to Jesus and was baptized in the river just a few days before he passed away.

Extra Vacation in Lusaka

As I mentioned before, the only link to the outside world that we had in Zaire was the daily 6:00 a.m. radio call from the Union. It would tell us mainly about the comings and goings of the three mission planes which were used to transport personnel in that vast territory. It was by this means of communication that I was called to be "ad interim" préfet and called to serve at Songa.

On May 11th, 1978 however, we heard that Congolese rebels were entering our southern border from Angola. They were called "Katangese" after the name of the region they had had to leave when Mobutu took power more than 20 years before. They had been refugees in Angola since that time, but Angola itself became independent from Portugal in 1975, and the two opposing party leaders, Savimbi and Neto, started a war that would last 27 years. In this turmoil, it was easy for the Katangese to gather weapons and start their own war against the president who had kicked them out. Now they were entering Zaire from the South—just where Songa is situated. It is also where the copper and diamonds mines are situated. They attacked Kolwezi, where hundreds of expatriates working in the mines were living. In a surprise attack on May 19th, 70 expatriates and hundreds of nationals were killed. You have to understand that Kolwezi was 150 km (95 miles) away and it was on the main road, just between us and the regional capital, Lubumbashi. The expected next move of the rebels was to go to Kamina, which was the only military base with an airport. Since it was a war situation with many casualties, it was expected that the rebels would need some medical assistance to care for their needs. Songa was the only "working" hospital at the time, with medicine and surgeons. Sick people came from thousands of kilometers away, to be treated at Songa! That was why our hospital had such a good reputation.

For our Union leaders, there was no doubt that Songa was to be the next target of the Katangese when they went up North. We were told by the Union on June 27, 1978, that each family had to be ready to leave that same day with one suitcase per family. Try to imagine for one minute what you would take with you if you had to leave for good. That gives you a good life lesson on what is important in your life and what is not! You will soon realize that most of the material things we have in life you can do without or replace except family pictures. Another decision I had to make on the fly: to whom should I give the school keys, the missionaries' houses, the safe, and everything else?

But the massacre in Kolwezi had triggered "Operation Kolwezi" led by the Belgian and French paratroopers to protect and evacuate the expatriates from that killing field. We drove to Kamina, and on the tarmac of Kamina's airport, a

Belgian army transport plane was waiting for us. It flew us to Lubumbashi where several vehicles from the Union awaited us to drive us down to Lusaka. We used the Union guest house, one family per room. Meanwhile, nothing serious happened in Songa and one month later, we had to return…to ask for our keys back! Miraculously nothing had been touched. Everything was exactly as we left it a month before. That in itself was another miracle in a country where things get "displaced' so easily!

Visit in the Middle of the Bush

Bob Lemon, the very same one who taught me the first rudiments of accounting in Lukanga, always took his job seriously. One morning we heard on the radio that he was planning to come to Songa. No specific dates were given, and we were told that he would arrange his own transportation from Lubumbashi to Songa! We were wondering what that meant because all missionaries and Union officials travelled by mission plane! Bob was born in Zaire to missionary parents. He spoke Kiswahili and managed to be understood in French. It turns out that he took the train from Lubumbashi to Kamina -a night trip that

I am sure he still remembers-, but the last part was even better. He borrowed a bicycle from the Conference office in Kamina and rode the 80 km on a sandy road with his suitcase on the baggage rack. On top of that, the pedals were not tightened properly and at each turn his right foot would have to catch up with the bearings. No need to say that when he arrived at Songa he was completely exhausted.

He was staying at our house, and before going to bed he took a bath. An hour later we had a flood in our bathroom. Bob fell asleep in the bath with the water tap open.

Yearend Grades
Ending up in Johannesburg

We somewhat managed to finish the school year and the day came when, as principal, I had to distribute the certificates to the students on the front porch of our house. One student who had completely failed his year thanked me by head-butting me on the nose…to the astonishment of the rest of the students who were wondering if they would get their certificates. It took me 10 minutes to clean the blood flowing from my broken nose, put a cotton plug in my nostril, change my shirt, and finish the ceremony that day. Guess what the topic of discussion was the next morning on the radio? Mannie Harcombe, the Union Treasurer, had to arrange a trip to Johannesburg for my nose to be fixed in a hospital. In fact, it was only three weeks later that I flew to Lubumbashi and the Union accountant, Leif, who was a South African himself, drove me down to Johannesburg. It was a three-day drive for more than 2,200 km; if we had had to drive to Kinshasa, almost the same distance, it would have taken us a month—if we could have found a road to drive on! So, it is thanks to England's former colonial ingenuity that we were able to cover that distance in only three days.

When one realizes that England had only around 10,000 people to develop the infra-structure of the subcontinent of

India, it was quite an accomplishment at the time!

On the way down South, since we were driving not far from it, I had the privilege of seeing the majestic Victoria Falls. It was a small consolation compared to the doctor's diagnosis when I arrived at the hospital: he had to break my nose again as it had set badly since its encounter with the student's head!

See you next time or adios?

By that time, it was our third year in the mission field and our furlough time had come. We were quite privileged since before that, it was every 6 years! We would not have dreamt that one day, missionaries would go on furlough every year!

We had sent our children ahead with Dr. Suzelle Vieilledent who was going on permanent return. She was a French doctor and agreed to take care of our children in advance of our furlough to France.

Notwithstanding the political situation in Zaire, it had been 8 months since we had left Lukanga and were still waiting for part of our goods to be sent to us. The mission planes were always too loaded to carry any of our stuff, and we were starting to wonder if the day would ever come when we would see them again. When we left, I wrote a letter to our Union asking them to take care of our goods during our two-month furlough. I thought that it was plenty of time, since during summer vacation there was less urgent business to deal with for our missionary planes. I never got an answer. While on furlough in our Division, there are two pilgrimages that one must make. The first is a relaxing 3-day medical checkup on the shore of Lake Leman at Clinique La Lignière, Switzerland. The second is a trip to Bern, Switzerland, to visit our leaders at the Division office. It is also a probing exam, but this time, not with medical instruments. Dr. Jean Zurcher, the former Director of our university in Collonges who baptized me in 1962 when I was in secondary school, was the Secretary of our Euro-Africa Division. And Pastor Edwin Ludesher, served as Division President. I had met him in 1969 when he was the president of the Union in the Cameroon when I spent a year as a volunteer.[9]

So, we were amongst friends. They wanted to know how things were going in these territories that they knew nothing about since it was outside the Division's territories. I told them part of the

---

[9] See pg. 27

adventures we went through and the fact that after having had to wait for 8 months for our goods from Europe to arrive at Lukanga, another 8 months had passed, and we were still waiting for part of our belongings! I mentioned the letter I had written to the Union officers and said that I was ready to move somewhere else if I did not get an answer. They expressed much concern and sympathy and asked me to stay in contact to make sure our problem was solved while at the same time telling me that we could always return to Africa, but in one of our Division territories. The months went by and at the end of the summer, not having received a word from our Union, I wrote to them that we were not returning to Songa. The Euro-Africa offered me a position as business manager at Nanga-Eboko Seminary in Cameroon for a year. They had further plans for me that I did not know about at the time.

I returned by myself to Songa a couple of months later to sell and give away the few things we had and shipped to Yaoundé the essential things that we wanted to keep.

Cameroon

We arrived in Yaoundé in late December 1978. It was just over nine years since I had landed in Yaoundé as a young volunteer.

This time there was a welcome committee at the airport to give us a lift to the Mission guest house. But we were a little disappointed when we disco-vered the next day that the rest of our trip to Nanga-Eboko, 130 km away, was to be made by rail! With two kids and our luggage this cooled down the first welcome we received. We were just wondering what other surprises were in store for us.

Marcel Fernandez, a schoolmate from Collonges and the school director there, was waiting for us at the station. That was nice! Since it was after 7 p.m. and already dark, he drove us directly to his house where we were surprised to meet the whole missionary family and share a meal together. Apart from the Fernandez family, they were all new faces. Several young single men who were spending their two-year mandatory French civil service as teachers in the secondary school, a couple of nurses taking care of the dispensary, and three professors at the theology school. The most memorable, however, was the maintenance man, Jacques Ritlewski, who was the clown of the group. His wife Babette was the school accountant. A life bond was created with them that very night. They are closer to me than my own siblings.

Regarding the housing aspect of our stay, I thought that we were back in Zaire when the Ahlers were expecting a new house upon their arrival. We were also told that we would live in a new house; it was not finished despite already having walls. We had to stay in the guest house for a couple of weeks before being able to move in. Even then the kitchen was not finished, and Eileen cooked in the garage for a couple of weeks.

Jean-Philippe had just turned 8 and it was high time that he started regular school. The previous year we had registered him and paid for primary school classes with Home Study International, our renowned school by correspondence. The only problem is that we never received the course! That is why, a year later, while waiting for our Cameroonian work visa, we had enrolled him in the French Ministry of Education distance learning program. Since we had been working mainly with American missionaries in Zaire, Eileen's French had not improved during the previous three years. We hired a theology student to help Jean-Philippe out with his lessons. We discovered later on that he was helping him so much that it was he who did Jean-Philippe's homework before they were sent for correction in France!

Douala

Before we left Europe, I had been told that the position in Nanga-Eboko was only temporary. It was such a pity because we liked Nanga so much that we could have spent the rest of our service, and lives for that matter, in that place. What our dear brethren from the Division had in mind though, was to send us to Douala where I was to serve as Secretary-Treasurer of the Field. The Division had decided that it was time to Africanize the leadership of the Church, and Jean-Claude Mongo had just been elected the first Cameroonian President of the West Cameroon Conference.

The only problem was that there was only one house belonging to the church in Douala. It was used by the former missionary president who had left on permanent return. The Division decided that we would use this house. As you can imagine that did not sit too well with the new president. We had to rent a house for him, while I built a new one behind the Douala church, which was on the same compound. It was a new house all right, but the prestige was in the old one. And we always felt the tension there.

We spent 5 years in Douala, during which time I inherited the Stewardship and Health Departments on top of my role as Secretary-Treasurer. Do you remember what I said about the French army?

We had a secondary school in Kribi and a dispensary in Buéa to take care of.

In Buéa, we had a missionary couple, Hans and Sylvie Obenhaus. She was a nurse taking care of the dispensary, and the revenue from that dispensary allowed me to build three churches during that time period (Bamenda, Edéa, and Douala Bassa). I used to go every week to take inventory and replenish the medicine since the dispensary was serving the community as the local pharmacy, as well.

Eileen was running the Book and Bible House, as well as doing the salaries for the Conference and taking care of the colporteurs. We had half a dozen of them, and business was brisk.

For the first time, Jean-Philippe and Sandrine could attend a regular school at the French school in Douala.

If we had some rare visitors in Zaire and Nanga-Eboko, we discovered that being the only missionary in Douala is like running a guest house.[10] Many visitors were in transit in Douala since it was the only international airport of the country at the time. We had a guest room that was rarely vacant. Our hospitality was well known even outside our church. It happened a few times that we had tourists who were travelling by motorbike or Land Rover who asked permission to pitch their tent in our garden, and they ended up in our guest room if it was free. Why? Only because

---

[10] We arrived in Douala June 28,1979. By the end of the year Eileen had served 82 meals to these hungry travelers, 25 of whom spent at least one night in our house.

when they were asking around about a place to spend the night on the cheap, people told them: "Go to the Adventist mission, they'll receive you." Even personnel at the airport were directing people who did not know where to go to our place. So, Eileen cooked a lot for brethren and strangers alike. Our children were used to giving up their beds for unexpected guests.

One time, Roy Terretta, who was in charge of the Publishing Department at the Union, thought it would be a great idea to invite Nigerian students to colporteur in order to earn their scholarship during the summer vacation, which encouraged a lot of the Cameroonian students to do the same. One day, we were told that 30 students would arrive in Douala. The day of their arrival, Eileen and some church ladies prepared food for them. Do you know how much food you need to feed 30 young men? It was a lot! And when the time came…the hard-working ladies waited, and waited, and waited some more until...they were told that they would not come that day! In Africa, especially in Douala, unless you have a huge fridge, which we did not have, it is impossible to keep food for too long. Eileen gave all the food away to the sisters who had come to help. They were "quite happy" about their day's work!

Then, on Friday afternoon just as the sun was setting, there was a ring at our gate and there stood 30 students! We had no food ready! What to do? Eileen let them in and, with a few quiet tears, set about calling in the sisters of the church and prepared food for these hungry students. What we had was more than enough. They stayed the night in the church and were on their way after Sabbath to begin their work.

We enjoyed our time in Douala, but as missionaries, we were by ourselves. As often as possible, when not hosting travelers of all sorts, we made the trip back to Nanga-Eboko for the weekend

Furlough

It was supposed to be a perfect summer. It was the first vacation that we had planned for ourselves. Previously, as missionaries, we had gone from one relative to another for our vacations but living out of suitcases with two children for two months at a time is not really fun after the first few days. For the first time, we decided that we would take two weeks to visit Ireland on our own.

I purchased a map and a Michelin Guide and mapped out where we would go and what we would see. We also decided where we would not go: Belfast, as at the time it was considered a war zone. Once the decision was taken, for us living on the equator in the heart of Africa, Ireland became the dreamland. Tickets were purchased, reservations made, and we were all living in anticipation of our D-day. For our children, the end of the school year could not come fast enough.

All seemed perfect until the Sunday before our departure. At the time, we were missionaries in Douala, the second most humid town on earth with a year-round 100% humidity factor and an average of 3.8 m (12,46 ft) of rainfall per year. Living on the mission compound behind the church, neither of our children needed much encouragement to use the old baptistery as a swimming pool.

As parents, we did not have the baptistry to distract us. It was much too small for us, and we still had to run the Mission's bookstore where Eileen was taking care of the colporteurs. That routine was broken by one of Eileen's requests. She asked me to fix a piece of equipment that my fellow American missionaries had not discovered the use for yet: a bidet. We used it for our washing machine outflow, and the bidet was leaking. I managed to dismantle it but as it was a Sunday, I did not have the right seal to fix it so I put it against the wall until the next day when I could buy the part needed and finish tinkering with it. Above the bidet was a clothesline. We had taught our children not to drop their swimming suits on the floor but to hang them on the clothesline.

In the afternoon after his daily dip in

the pool, Jean- Philippe, then ten years old, being a good boy as he was, went into the bathroom to hang his swim trunks on the clothesline. As usual, he climbed on the bidet not paying attention to the fact that this time it was no longer fixed to the ground. And here went our Irish vacation. The bidet skidded, Jean-Philippe fell on it breaking the porcelain in a thousand pieces and cutting through our son's groin. It was our daughter's shouts that made us run to the bathroom to watch our son with blood gushing from his groin. The cut was 5cm long and the artery was severed. I took a towel and exerted pressure on the wound, grabbed him, and lay him on the back seat of our car to rush him to find a hospital with a surgeon on duty on a Sunday afternoon in Africa! We knew that time was of the essence, but under the shock, I did not know where to go, although there was a small clinic near our mission compound.

Eileen, who under normal circumstances is unable to tell right from left when she is driving, was giving me directions. We usually ask her to guide us when we have time and want to visit places that we have never been to and never had the intention of visiting. But that day while applying all her efforts to put pressure on that terrible wound, she directed me to the nearby small clinic.

As it was a Sunday, only a nurse was on duty at the desk. I called for a stretcher and asked him to urgently call the surgeon. But he sternly told me that procedures had to be followed! In such a case the nurse on duty had to see for himself if the surgeon was to be called! That meant that I had to release the pressure on Jean-Philippe's wound with a consequence that is easy to imagine. I started shouting at him, I am sure it was an occasion for him to enrich his French vocabulary, that attracted another nurse to come who assessed the situation in one glance and immediately called the surgeon who arrived several minutes later. Jean-Philippe was white as a sheet when he entered the theater. After surgery, the doctor told us that it had been a matter of minutes between life and death, we could have lost him. He was well, but since they did not have time to do a blood test, they had to give him whatever blood they had on hand, and it ended up not being his blood type. The bad news was that his crural nerve was severed and that he would never be able to walk properly.

We were thankful that God had saved his life but were overly concerned about his future. No need to say that we were ready to forget our nice holiday in Ireland to consult the best neurosurgeon possible to have a second opinion and see if anything could be done to give Jean-Philippe a chance to walk normally.

Our detailed plans were turned into flight cancellations and the next two months were to be spent in relatives' homes in France, but we were so relieved and happy that Jean-Philippe was still with us.

He needed crutches to walk as he

could not move his right leg. The specialist in Lyon had a long waiting list. Fortunately, through a cousin working in the University Hospital in Geneva, we managed to have an appointment with the best neurosurgeon, who was also a Professor at the University.

After running a battery of tests including an electromyography to test his nerve activity, he could only confirm the verdict of his colleague in Douala, the crural nerve was severed. However, contrary to the other doctor, he said that he could perform a graft with a section of Jean-Philippe's nerve in the lower part of his leg. We were so happy to hear that there was a chance of a cure for Jean-Philippe's situation.

The downside of it was that he would

not know if the graft had worked until a year later as a nerve had to rebuild its connection at the rate of one centimeter per year! That was the only procedure that he knew of. The surgeon explained to us that nerves are like stretched elastic bands, when you cut one, both ends retract. The recovery process itself was going to be along. That meant that Jean-Philippe would be OK…in a few years.

Before doing the nerve graft, however, another one had to take place. The surgeon in Douala had just stuck a large self-adhering plastic bandage over our son's wound and a large hematoma had developed and damaged the cut that he had in his groin. A skin graft had to be done to clean up the wound before the nerve graft could take place. The skin graft took place the following day and we had to wait a few weeks for that wound to be dry and healthy in order for the nerve graft to be done. All the church members in Thonon, our local church, were praying for him.

In September, when the nerve graft was due as planned, we checked Jean-Philippe in, the day before the operation at Geneva University Hospital. Jean-Philippe was such a unique case that the surgeon took his students to our son's room. In explaining the case and showing the electromyogram results, he asked Jean-Philippe to try moving his toes to show the students that there was not any nerve reaction. But to the amazement of all, Jean-Philippe mana-ged to move some of his toes. The surgeon could not explain it and in front of his students he said, "only the Holy Spirit could have done that." Surgery was cancelled to let the natural recovery process take place. We were to check Jean-Philippe's condition a year later. That we did, and although we might have felt that God took his own time…the miracle was confirmed. Even the surgeon could not explain Jean-Philippe's regaining the function of his right leg without the nerve graft.

The surgeon, knowing that we were missionaries, did not charge us any fees. He said that we had paid enough for airline tickets to bring him to Geneva. This was clearly a miracle and a great witness to the surgeon and his staff.

Do you still not believe in miracles?

Moving

Moving is part of a pastor's life. Do you know how many times you moved in your life? I do – we moved 9 times during our ministry and 7 times before that. But since we are a part of the Adventist movement, moving is part of our genes.

At the time, our good friend Karl Johnson was a theology professor at the school at Nanga-Eboko. He told us that his father, also a pastor, had a saying:

There are three things that a pastor should always be ready to do:

1. To preach
2. To move
3. To die.

I can vouch for the first two and am waiting for the third.

We were to move from Douala to Yaoundé to the Union office as I had been called to serve as Associate-Treasurer of the Union.

We had driven that road many times before, but at the time it was a dirt road which, during the rainy season, could take up to 5 hours to arrive in Yaoundé. The new road had recently been finished. It is not a long one, 180 km (112 miles), but a crucial one, since it is the link between the only harbor of the country, Douala, the economic capital, and the legislative capital. That road had been paid for three times already by the French government, who repeatedly made the same mistake: they gave the money to the government. With the result that nothing happened. The fourth time, (who said that the French people are slow to learn?), it contracted a company to do the job and paid it directly.

We had a new paved road. And we were going to enjoy our trip to Yaoundé. We had sent our children in advance with friends to make sure we had the house to ourselves to pack our things. The truck was loaded, and we sent it on its way.

We stayed the night at the Procure's guest house, and we took our time. We had a good breakfast to start with and around 9, we took off.

It was about noon when we reached the neighborhood of Yaoundé. We were quite surprised that the traffic was thinning.

We were moving along rapidly, when the car in front of us made a sudden turn in the middle of the road and went sideways to stop on the side of the road. I shook my head at these crazy taxi drivers who had "negotiated" their driving license on the side of the road. But suddenly we heard a noise that we never heard before. The car shuddered and somebody was waving at us. We were in the suburb and a guy in uniform with his machine-gun was hiding behind a tree. His signs were quite clear: we had to get off the road. This time I shook my head at these crazy soldiers who could have found a better day to exercise than the day we were moving. Then we realized that there were a whole bunch of them scattered everywhere. We were near the National Radio Station which explained the number of soldiers along the road. I drove off the road not knowing where I was going. There were not a lot of people around to ask. It was the middle of the day and usually these places were swarming with people! After a long detour, I finally arrived at a crossing that I recognized, and we made our way to the Adventist Publishing House where we were expected.

Upon driving our car into the parking lot, I realized that my front left tire was flat. Our hosts greeted us with concern. And we discovered that we had driven in the middle of a "coup d'état." The former president was trying to oust the newly elected one and the soldiers we saw were not just exercising, but they were fighting against the rebels and defending the National Radio and TV Station. I checked my tire, and lo and behold, it was flat because a bullet had gone right through it and ended up in the AC system. But the tire held enough air to arrive at the mission before collapsing completely. A second bullet was embedded in the door frame of the car. Had it gone through, my left ankle would have been shattered?

We spent the following week in the Treasurer's apartment at the Union office. Nobody was allowed outside as bands of rebels and soldiers were playing hide and seek on the Union compound. The nights were spent in the corridor in the middle of the apartment, the only safe place where we were protected from bullets. That reminded us of Lukanga when we also had time to inspect every inch of our corridor for one night.

But best of all, we had lost contact with the driver of our truck. Remember, no cell phone at the time! After several days of waiting, we thought that we could say goodbye to our belongings. But one week later, surprise surprise, the driver showed up with all our goods. Nothing was missing. He had hidden his truck somewhere in the suburb out of sight of any prying eyes.

What were you saying about miracles?

Back to France

After eight years of service in Cameroon we returned to France for good. The choice was essentially made for the good of our children's education. The French schools in either Douala or Yaoundé were good, but the vast majority of their schoolmates were not exactly coming from our background. Most students were children of expatriates who were directors of large international businesses or banks, or owners of large local companies. As our children were often invited to their friends' houses, they could easily see that their lifestyle was a bit different than ours, to say the least.

Upon our return to Europe in 1986,

our Division brethren had another surprise for me. They had a plan that I did not know anything about, but before it could be executed, they offered me a scholarship to study computer science at Webster University in Geneva.

For this reason, they asked our Campus in Collonges to find an apartment for us. Jean-Philippe and Sandrine could start their regular school year on campus, which was our priority. First, I did not understand why they were asking me to take the computer course. Can you imagine what computer science was like in 1986? It was not too far from the Abacus! The year before, as I was the business manager of our printing press in Yaoundé, I managed to ask a friend who was the manager of our Publishing House in France, "Vie et Santé," to purchase a Commodore 64 and send it to me in Yaoundé. I had the weird idea at the time of computerizing the accounting of the Imprimerie de la Mission Adventiste (IMA). It took a couple of months to get there, but by the time I played with it a little bit, I realized that there was nothing I could do without a program! Nobody told me that we needed specific software to run this machine! I thought that you could just type some commands and voilà! It was a 6-bit computer with a floppy disc and was the bestselling computer at the time, and there was nothing I could do with it! Our iPhones today have probably a thousand times more memory and work a thousand times faster than my Commodore! When the teenage son of Roy Terretta, the Publishing Director of the Union, heard that we had a computer, he rushed to IMA and in playing with it, soon discovered how to play an electronic ping pong game. He was probably the predecessor of millions of kids glued to their screen for hours on end.

Had our brethren heard of my success in computerizing IMA and decided that I needed a little, I mean, serious, help?

My scholarship was extended for a second year to complete an MBA since it took only two semesters more to do it. In fact, they were giving me the opportunity to earn a degree for the job I had been doing for the last 10 years!

It was at the end of March 1988 that our brethren's plan was revealed.

Maurice Zehnacker, who was the Business Manager of our Seminary in France, was elected President of our Union and was to move to Paris…leaving his seat empty! It was really fortunate that I was just there to fill in! That is what planning was for, my friend! The plan was that I would computerize the accounting system of Collonges, and incidentally manage the school as well.

It was a long and painful process for some of the employees. The younger ones were eager to change over, but for those almost at retirement age…it was different! At the time, the only off-the-shelf accounting programs were for quite simple businesses. The Campus at Collonges had four different schools which had to be integrated within the same software which had to be written specifically for us.

While managing this transition between the Middle Ages in accounting and Modern Times, I also took care of other issues on campus.

It did not take me long to notice that the expenses incurred by the cafeteria were well over the income. I was wondering why. In going to my office one Sunday morning, I saw one of the cooks, loading his car with boxes of vegetables and food items. Since it was the cooks who had to go to the market at least once a week to purchase vegetables and food items I did not pay attention at that moment. Later in the day, however, I called the chief cook and asked where his colleague was that day. The answer he gave me was what I feared: he was visiting his parents that day! Here was the origin of our deficit.

I had a choice to make, raise a ruckus firing a cook, which meant hunting for another one SDA patented, etc., etc., or finding another solution. Do you know what is the main subject of dissatisfaction in a school? The food! Thinking about the business of running a kitchen, making all purchases, balancing not only the budget but also the diet of dozens of students and visitors, and trying to please everybody is not easy. It did not take me long to decide that I did not want to be involved in the daily nitty gritty of that responsibility. I looked around, made some inquiries, and decided to outsource our cafeteria.

You can imagine that I had a lot of push back against it. It had never been done before in one of our institutions! What kind of food were these heathen people going to feed our children? Etc., etc. As one saying goes, "They sang The Marseillaise to me in Portuguese." I had first to convince our board, then our personnel. But the numbers were there to support that decision. If we had no say in whom the company chose to run the cafeteria for us, there were, nonetheless, conditions:

1. All cooks were to go first to a culinary school to take vegetarian cooking for three weeks.

2. The company would take care of all purchasing, as well as the cooks' salaries and compensations.

3. We would be charged by a system of points on food items sold.

4. Students were allotted a number of points per trimester and could even invite their visiting parents or friends to eat with them on their account, if they had enough points. That had never been allowed before.

Not only did we remain under budget, but the kitchen was a small source of profit for the first time in decades. Is that not what a manager is supposed to do: turn a cost center into a profit center?

More than 30 years later it is still outsourced.

Beating the Inflation to Our Benefit

In the late 1980s, we were living in a recession with an inflation rate above 10%. The traditional way of paying our bills at Collonges was…to pay them as soon as they arrived. We were very good customers and were appreciated by the local merchants.

However, because of the high inflation rate, banks developed a financial tool which was called Sicav at the time, by which you could invest your money on a short-term basis with a return which was just 1 or 2 points below the inflation rate. It was available on a daily basis and was sort of a piggy bank that you could go to anytime you wanted to.

I decided to use that tool and put all our cash in that special account. Instead of paying our suppliers on a daily basis as soon we received their invoice, we waited for the official time allowed: most were on a 30-day period, although some for 90 days.

By the end of the year, we had an additional income of over 200,000 French francs that we never had before!

Language Courses

Switzerland was not hit as hard financially as we were in the rest of Europe. Geneva, which was just 10 km across the border, was still attracting a lot of people looking for good paying jobs.

It was at that time that the mayor of Archamps, a nearby village, wanting to piggyback on the booming economy in Geneva, had the idea of developing an International Business Park.

It was supposed to attract international companies to compete with Geneva with the advantage of much lower costs as far as offices and labor costs were concerned.

However, to work for an international company, you needed to be fluent at least in English. That gave me the idea of developing night language courses for adults. We had three levels in English and, for good measure, since we had the qualified personnel for it, in Spanish and German, as well. It was quite successful since we had around 120 students coming from all walks of life mixing together. At the end of each course, we had a celebration with a small buffet, and people enjoyed spending time together. We even had the local baker's wife attending our Spanish course. This gave the occasion for the local people to come for time on campus, to talk with us, and to discover that up high on our mountain, we Seventh-day Adventists were not strange people after all.

Missionaries in Switzerland

Does that title bother you? It does seem a bit strange when you are living in one of the richest countries in the world. But don't we call *missionaries* people working outside of their homeland? When our pioneers came to Switzerland from the United States in the late 1880's, they were called "missionaries." And today's Mormons going for a stint of two years of service abroad or at home are called missionaries.

It so happened that in early 1993, our Division in Bern called me to be an Associate Treasurer.

I was assigned the Latin countries of our Division: France, Italy, Spain, Portugal, Romania, plus several others: Czechoslovakia (at the time one country, now separated and forming the Czech and Slovak republics), Bulgaria, and last but not least, Angola and Mozambique. There were not many countries left apart from Switzerland and Germany!

We were in the early 90's and it was the time of Perestroika, and a lot was happening on the Eastern front! The Berlin Wall had fallen and Ceausescu, the Romanian dictator, had been overthrown, imprisoned, and executed for high treason.

Upon my arrival, since I did not have too much in my portfolio (!), the brethren asked me to devote 10% of my time to auditing. And the first ones I had to do were in Romania!

You have to understand that the Church in Romania was not officially recognized but were tolerated under the Communist regime. There were spies coming into the churches to report to the government names of pastors, leaders, and any worthy bit of information a Communist regime may be interested in. The government knew that we were collecting money! In accordance, our brethren knew that there were people reporting them and they acted accordingly! That means that they had two sets of accounts: one official and one real. The only problem is that I had a hard time matching the numbers I had to deal with in the ledger and the cost of living.

On my first trip to Bucharest the treasurer welcomed me in his Dacia, a local copy of the Renault 12. He stopped on the way to my hotel to get some gas, because he noticed a line forming in a gas station. Gas was scarce and every opportunity was taken to fill up. I happened to see how much he had to pay for it. It was only a couple days later that I realized that he had paid a full month's salary just to fill up his tank! Then I learned that every pastor had a car that represented 20 years' salary! I started asking questions and finally they told me that some received help from family members living in West-ern Europe, but in most cases, it was the church members who had purchased a car for their pastor, who would have been financially unable to do so. It dawned on me that there was quite a bit of "creative" accounting going on. What was I supposed to do? I was the first auditor they had seen in 40 years! The Treasurer, a designated pastor who had accepted the challenge to be Union Treasurer, managed to build a 500-seat church under Ceausescu, al-though at the time it was forbidden to do so! In fact, during our round of auditing in the country, he insisted that we make quite a detour to show me the famous church he built since a wedding was taking place there that Sunday.

I immediately suspected that it was a diversion from the auditing that I was supposed to perform in one of the Conferences.

However, he was the host and visiting

his church…etc., etc., I could not refuse. He just called in advance to tell the local leader that we were on our way. When we arrived at the church, I discovered that what he had not told me was that I was supposed to do the blessing on the new couple. I had 10 minutes to prepare, find a tie and…perform. Do you remember the three things that a pastor…

Angola and Mozambique

Angola and Mozambique are Portuguese speaking countries on each side of Africa. Angola on the west coast, Mozambique on the southeast side. These countries have been at war since the 1960s when they first started to fight to oust Portugal, which had been their colonial power, and when that was achieved in the 1970s, they continued to fight among themselves to gain control of the government. In the early 1990s, because of this situation, these countries had never been audited.

During my time at the Division office, I would spend almost a month every year bet-ween these two African countries.

If Mozambique was almost at peace, Angola, on the other hand, was still divided. Flying to Luanda, Angola's capital city, was not a problem. However, our Union office was in Huambo. It was situated squarely in the middle of the country, and all the surrounding areas were still controlled by Unita, whose leader Savimbi had his private home in Huambo. To say that he was eager to "liberate" his hometown was a euphemism. Dr. Stoeger, the Director of our Health Department in Bern had experienced how close the rebels were when they shot at his plane which was taking off. Nobody was hurt but I saw the wreckage of his Boing 727 off the side of the runway when I flew in for the first time.

Since that incident, no regular airlines wanted to fly to Huambo. The courageous ones had to take an old Ilyushin, Russian plane that was most certainly a remain-der of equipment sent by Russia in the 70s to help their friends fight the colonialists.

The pilot was Russian and had to be paid in cash. The first flight that I took, I had to share the seat with a robust Mama who had a couple of chickens on her knees. I didn't complain because further down the cabin, another passenger had a goat as companion. The flight was almost eventless until we arrived over Huambo. The rebels were close by and the only way to land at Huambo was to fly high over the city and to come down in a tight spiral in order to land out of range of the rebels' weapons. If you have tried a merry-go-round at Disney World, it is the same—but multiply it by ten times.

The procedure for takeoff is exactly the same until the plane reaches an altitude safe enough to fly level. On my departure the plane was shaking so badly that the exit signs were falling off their placements, the overhead bins were flying open, and to crown it all, the pilot cabin door flew open…and an empty bottle of Vodka rolled all along the cabin to the toilet at the end. You may think that an African's face turns green when he is afraid; it is not true—they were all grey.

There was no hotel to go to, I was to stay at the Treasurer's house. Auditing in such conditions is a bit…difficult to say the least. What I first noticed is that, according to the church records, there had not been one death since the beginning of the conflict had begun more than thirty years before. They had had, however, a lot of baptisms. I supposed that it gave me a glimpse into how records were kept in Angola.

As I talked to a lot of people, they all came to see the white man. I heard a few complaints about how that church was managed, and some brethren even showed me a brand-new house that the Treasurer had recently built. It was a brick-and-mortar house, not a thatched roof hut. If salaries in Romania were about $200 a month for a pastor, they were much lower in Angola. The conclusion had to be made, there were some leaks that I had to find. It did not take long to find them—but then what?

As you can imagine, contacting the Division was a little tricky in the middle of the bush. The Union office had one phone that worked from time to time, but getting an international line was by pure chance. On top of that, to have a private discussion with our leaders when half a dozen persons surrounded you was…difficult. I could speak French but several of our leaders spoke that language. I could have tried the little German I knew, but the Union Secretary got his education at Friedensau, our Seminary in Germany when it was under Communist rule. I managed to contact the Division Treasurer in English and explained the situation using covert language. He asked me to call him back the following day because he needed to consult with the other officers.

I did, and the answer was very simple: have the President call an emergency Union Committee meeting and have the Treasurer removed from his position!

That was easy to say, but convincing our African brothers to *fire* him was not a simple task. It was done by stressing greatly that the Division, which was supporting the Union financially for... everything, could not continue sending subsidies and equipment on a yearly basis to an administration which was not appreciative of the brethren in Europe who were so supportive of them.

Fortunately, I had planned that Union

meeting the day prior to my departure for one good reason: the Treasurer was my host, and he was feeding me during my sojourn! Do you understand why, pretending stomach trouble, I skipped dinner and breakfast after he was demoted?

Epilogue

I will stop reminiscing here about our African experiences which happened during the time we were serving in Berne for the Euro-Africa Division.

We have some other ones in a different context and maybe one day…

I sent a copy of this manuscript to a longtime friend whose father had been for 10 years a missionary in Cameroon. His reaction to reading the pages that you just read surprised me a little bit. In acknowledging the fact that several situations that we had lived reminded stories that his father told him about when he was young, he simply asked me if it was good thing to tell *everything*?

So, I decided to send another copy to another longtime friend and colleague, who went through some of the same experiences we had in Zaire.

His reaction was completely different. He reminded me of the Mission Institute we went through before leaving for Africa in 1975. This seminar was essentially to demystify all the preconceived ideas we may have had on missions in general. And to be ready for some surprises when we would have to confront the reality of the situation. The purpose of the institute was to prevent us from leaving our country with rosy ideas about the mission field that might be shattered as soon as we would set foot "abroad".

We were told by the witnesses of the following situation. A new missionary couple was expected at Gitwe, our school in Rwanda. The day of their arrival, everybody was dumbstruck to see the car carrying the new missionaries drive around the campus and leave to return to the capital city, not even bothering to stop! From there, the missionaries of a few hours left to return home. What they saw probably did not match what their ideas were! All these expenses were, of course, paid by the church! I don't know who recruited this couple, but if our leaders had been a bit more forthcoming about the realty of the situation, that experience, and the costs incurred by it, could have been avoided.

Another less consequential story is the following. A missionary family arrived all by themselves as expatriates at one of those mission stations that were lost in the bush. Sometime later, their fridge stopped working. In fact, the whole house had no electricity. They were the only ones who had that commodity in their vicinity. The only problem was that our brother, who was a good pastor, had absolutely no practical sense at all. If he had discovered the fuse box in a corner of the house, he still would have had no idea how to fix the problem, so he had to call an electrician from the nearest town, a day's travel away, to change their fuse.

For those readers who might be shocked or embarrassed, please excuse my forwardness.

It doesn't change the fact that the main topic of this book is about God's multiple miraculous interventions during our missionary experience, in difficult even dangerous situations. May His name be glorified for that!

Acknowledgment

To Eileen, my rock. I am always astonished after more than 50 years of marriage; she still bears with me. Not only did she experience (undergo!) all these situations while a keeping good spirit, but in a real missionary attitude, accepted all sort of jobs—although she was not trained for them—from teaching English, to being dean in a girls dorm in Zaire, to being accountant and book shop manager in Cameroon, to being assistant librarian in France.

She reminded me of some of the episodes related in this book and then corrected not only details, but also the

English version of this book. I love you, Babe!

To Jean-Philippe, our son, who spent countless hours formatting and transferring the manuscript. Without his work, you wouldn't be reading these lines.

To Sandrine, our daughter, who was 3 years old when we left for Zaire and remembers some of the situations we lived through together, and who, with her daughter, **Amélie**, had "fun" correcting the French version of this book.

To Vanessa, our "baby," who was not born until four years after our return to Europe, but who, in correcting this book, learned quite a bit about what Maman and Papa were up to on the African continent!

To Laren and **Averil Kurtz**, companions d'armes, French speaking since…always. We met in Zaire, then they went as missionaries to Mexico, but remained fluent and active in Molière's tongue. They revisited my French version.

© 2023 Jean-Luc Lézeau
Publisher: BoD - Books on Demand, info@bod.fr
Printing: BoD - Books on Demand, In de
Tarpen 42, Norderstedt (Germany)
Print on demand
ISBN: 978-2-3224-7381-6
Legal deposit: Juin 2023